Travel phrasebooks collection
«Everything Will Be Okay!»

T&P Books Publishing

CW00925030

PHRASEBOOK

- ROMANIAN -

THE MOST IMPORTANT PHRASES

This phrasebook contains the most important phrases and questions for basic communication
Everything you need to survive overseas

By Andrey Taranov

T&P BOOKS

Phrasebook + 250-word dictionary

English-Romanian phrasebook & mini dictionary

By Andrey Taranov

The collection of "Everything Will Be Okay" travel phrasebooks published by T&P Books is designed for people traveling abroad for tourism and business. The phrasebooks contain what matters most - the essentials for basic communication. This is an indispensable set of phrases to "survive" while abroad.

You'll also find a mini dictionary with 250 useful words required for everyday communication - the names of months and days of the week, measurements, family members, and more.

T&P Books Publishing
www.tpbooks.com

ISBN: 978-1-78492-410-2

This book is also available in E-book formats.
Please visit www.tpbooks.com or the major online bookstores.

FOREWORD

The collection of "Everything Will Be Okay" travel phrasebooks published by T&P Books is designed for people traveling abroad for tourism and business. The phrasebooks contain what matters most - the essentials for basic communication. This is an indispensable set of phrases to "survive" while abroad.

This phrasebook will help you in most cases where you need to ask something, get directions, find out how much something costs, etc. It can also resolve difficult communication situations where gestures just won't help.

This book contains a lot of phrases that have been grouped according to the most relevant topics. You'll also find a mini dictionary with useful words - numbers, time, calendar, colors...

Take "Everything Will Be Okay" phrasebook with you on the road and you'll have an irreplaceable traveling companion who will help you find your way out of any situation and teach you to not fear speaking with foreigners.

TABLE OF CONTENTS

T&P Books Publishing

PRONUNCIATION

T&P phonetic alphabet	Romanian example	English example
[a]	arbust [ar'bust]	shorter than in ask
[e]	a merge [a 'merdʒe]	elm, medal
[ə]	brățară [brə'tsarə]	Schwa, rediced 'e'
[i]	impozit [im'pozit]	shorter than in feet
[ɨ]	cuvânt [ku'vɨnt]	big, America
[o]	avocat [avo'kat]	pod, John
[u]	fluture ['fluture]	book
[b]	bancă ['bankə]	baby, book
[d]	durabil [du'rabil]	day, doctor
[dʒ]	gemeni ['dʒemenʲ]	joke, general
[f]	frizer [fri'zer]	face, food
[g]	gladiolă [gladi'olə]	game, gold
[ʒ]	jucător [ʒukə'tor]	forge, pleasure
[h]	pahar [pa'har]	home, have
[k]	actor [ak'tor]	clock, kiss
[l]	clopot ['klopot]	lace, people
[m]	mobilă ['mobilə]	magic, milk
[n]	nuntă ['nuntə]	name, normal
[p]	profet [pro'fet]	pencil, private
[r]	roată [ro'atə]	rice, radio
[s]	salată [sa'latə]	city, boss
[ʃ]	cleștișor [kleʃtiˈʃor]	machine, shark
[t]	statuie [sta'tue]	tourist, trip
[ts]	forță ['fortsə]	cats, tsetse fly
[tʃ]	optzeci [opt'zetʃi]	church, French
[v]	valiză [va'lizə]	very, river
[z]	zmeură ['zmeurə]	zebra, please
[j]	foios [fo'jos]	yes, New York
[ʲ]	zori [zorʲ]	palatalization sign

LIST OF ABBREVIATIONS

English abbreviations

ab.	-	about
adj	-	adjective
adv	-	adverb
anim.	-	animate
as adj	-	attributive noun used as adjective
e.g.	-	for example
etc.	-	et cetera
fam.	-	familiar
fem.	-	feminine
form.	-	formal
inanim.	-	inanimate
masc.	-	masculine
math	-	mathematics
mil.	-	military
n	-	noun
pl	-	plural
pron.	-	pronoun
sb	-	somebody
sing.	-	singular
sth	-	something
v aux	-	auxiliary verb
vi	-	intransitive verb
vi, vt	-	intransitive, transitive verb
vt	-	transitive verb

Romanian abbreviations

f	-	feminine noun
f pl	-	feminine plural
m	-	masculine noun
m pl	-	masculine plural
n	-	neuter
n pl	-	neuter plural
pl	-	plural

ROMANIAN PHRASEBOOK

This section contains important phrases that may come in handy in various real-life situations.
The phrasebook will help you ask for directions, clarify a price, buy tickets, and order food at a restaurant

T&P Books Publishing

PHRASEBOOK
CONTENTS

T&P Books Publishing

Excuse me, ...	**Nu vă supărați, ...** [nu və supə'rats^j, ...]
Hello.	**Buna ziua.** [buna 'ziwa]
Thank you.	**Mulțumesc.** [multsu'mesk]
Good bye.	**La revedere.** [la reve'dere]
Yes.	**Da.** [da]
No.	**Nu.** [nu]
I don't know.	**Nu știu.** [nu 'ʃtiu]
Where? | Where to? | When?	**Unde? | Încotro? | Când?** [unde? | inko'tro? | kind?]

I need ...	**Am nevoie de ...** [am ne'voje de ...]
I want ...	**Vreau ...** [vr^jau ...]
Do you have ...?	**Aveți ...?** [a'vets^j ...?]
Is there a ... here?	**Există ... aici?** [e'gzistə ... a'itʃi?]
May I ...?	**Pot ...?** [pot ...?]
..., please (polite request)	**..., vă rog** [..., və rog]

I'm looking for ...	**Caut ...** [kaut ...]
the restroom	**o toaletă** [o toa'letə]
an ATM	**un bancomat** [un banko'mat]
a pharmacy (drugstore)	**o farmacie** [o farma'tʃie]
a hospital	**un spital** [un spi'tal]
the police station	**o secție de poliție** [o 'sektsie de po'litsie]
the subway	**un metrou** [un me'trou]

a taxi	**un taxi** [un ta'ksi]
the train station	**o gară** [o 'garə]

My name is ...	**Numele meu este ...** [numele 'meu 'este ...]
What's your name?	**Cum vă numiți?** [kum və nu'mitsʲ?]
Could you please help me?	**Mă puteți ajuta, vă rog?** [mə pu'tetsʲ aʒu'ta, və rog?]
I've got a problem.	**Am o problemă.** [am o pro'blemə]
I don't feel well.	**Mi-e rău.** [mi-e 'rəu]
Call an ambulance!	**Chemați o ambulanță!** [ke'matsʲ o ambu'lantsə!]
May I make a call?	**Pot să dau un telefon?** [pot sə dau un tele'fon?]

I'm sorry.	**Îmi pare rău.** [ɨmʲ 'pare rəu]
You're welcome.	**Cu plăcere.** [ku plə'tʃere]

I, me	**Eu** [eu]
you (inform.)	**tu** [tu]
he	**el** [el]
she	**ea** [ja]
they (masc.)	**ei** [ej]
they (fem.)	**ele** ['ele]
we	**noi** [noj]
you (pl)	**voi** [voj]
you (sg, form.)	**dumneavoastră** [dumnʲavo'astrə]

ENTRANCE	**INTRARE** [in'trare]
EXIT	**IEȘIRE** [je'ʃire]
OUT OF ORDER	**DEFECT** [de'fekt]
CLOSED	**ÎNCHIS** [ɨn'kis]

OPEN	**DESCHIS** [des'kis]
FOR WOMEN	**PENTRU FEMEI** [pentru fe'mej]
FOR MEN	**PENTRU BĂRBAȚI** [pentru ber'batsʲ]

Questions

Where?	**Unde?** ['unde?]
Where to?	**Încotro?** [ɨnko'tro?]
Where from?	**De unde?** [de 'unde?]
Why?	**De ce?** [de tʃe?]
For what reason?	**Din ce motiv?** [din tʃe mo'tiv?]
When?	**Când?** [kɨnd?]
How long?	**Cât?** [kɨt?]
At what time?	**La ce oră?** [la tʃe 'orə?]
How much?	**Cât de mult?** [kɨt de mult?]
Do you have ...?	**Aveți ...?** [a'vetsʲ ...?]
Where is ...?	**Unde este ...?** [unde 'este ...?]
What time is it?	**Cât este ceasul?** [kɨt 'este 'tʃasul?]
May I make a call?	**Pot să dau un telefon?** [pot sə dau un tele'fon?]
Who's there?	**Cine e?** [tʃine e?]
Can I smoke here?	**Pot fuma aici?** [pot fu'ma a'itʃi?]
May I ...?	**Pot ...?** [pot ...?]

Needs

I'd like ...	**Aş dori ...** [aʃ do'ri ...]
I don't want ...	**Nu vreau ...** [nu 'vrʲau ...]
I'm thirsty.	**Mi-e sete.** [mi-e 'sete]
I want to sleep.	**Vreau să dorm.** [vrʲau sə dorm]
I want ...	**Vreau ...** [vrʲau ...]
to wash up	**să mă spăl** [sə mə spəl]
to brush my teeth	**să mă spăl pe dinţi** [sə mə spəl pe 'dintsi]
to rest a while	**să mă odihnesc puţin** [sə mə odih'nesk pu'tsin]
to change my clothes	**să mă schimb** [sə mə skimb]
to go back to the hotel	**să mă întorc la hotel** [sə mə ɨn'tork la ho'tel]
to buy ...	**să cumpăr ...** [sə 'kumpər ...]
to go to ...	**să merg la ...** [sə merg la ...]
to visit ...	**să vizitez ...** [sə vizi'tez ...]
to meet with ...	**să mă întâlnesc cu ...** [sə mə ɨntɨl'nesk ku ...]
to make a call	**să dau un telefon** [sə dau un tele'fon]
I'm tired.	**Sunt obosit /obosită/.** [sunt obo'sit /obo'sitə/]
We are tired.	**Suntem obosiţi.** [suntem obo'sitsi]
I'm cold.	**Mi-e frig.** [mi-e frig]
I'm hot.	**Mi-e cald.** [mi-e kald]
I'm OK.	**Sunt bine.** [sunt 'bine]

I need to make a call.	**Trebuie să dau un telefon.** [trebuje sə dau un tele'fon]
I need to go to the restroom.	**Trebuie să merg la toaletă.** [trebuje sə merg la toa'letə]
I have to go.	**Chiar trebuie să plec.** [kjar 'trebuje sə plek]
I have to go now.	**Trebuie să plec.** [trebuje sə plek]

Asking for directions

Excuse me, ...	**Nu vă supărați, ...** [nu və supə'ratsʲ, ...]
Where is ...?	**Unde este ...?** [unde 'este ...?]
Which way is ...?	**În ce direcție este ...?** [in tʃe di'rektsie 'este ...?]
Could you help me, please?	**Ați putea să mă ajutați, vă rog?** [atsʲ put'a sə mə aʒu'tatsʲ, və rog?]

I'm looking for ...	**Caut ...** [kaut ...]
I'm looking for the exit.	**Caut ieșirea.** [kaut 'eʃirʲa]
I'm going to ...	**Urmează să ...** [ur'mʲazə sə ...]
Am I going the right way to ...?	**Merg în direcția bună către ...?** [merg in di'rektsja 'bunə 'kɛtre ...?]

Is it far?	**Este departe?** [este de'parte?]
Can I get there on foot?	**Pot ajunge acolo pe jos?** [pot a'ʒunʒe a'kolo pe ʒos?]
Can you show me on the map?	**Îmi puteți arăta pe hartă?** [imʲ pu'tetsʲ arə'ta pe 'hartə?]
Show me where we are right now.	**Arătați-mi unde ne aflăm acum.** [arə'tatsi-mi 'unde ne afləm a'kum]

Here	**Aici** [a'itʃi]
There	**Acolo** [a'kolo]
This way	**Pe aici** [pe a'itʃi]

Turn right.	**Faceți dreapta.** [fa'tʃetsʲ 'drʲapta]
Turn left.	**Faceți stânga.** [fa'tʃetsʲ 'stinga]
first (second, third) turn	**prima (a doua, a treia)** [prima (a 'dowa, a 'treja)]
to the right	**la dreapta** [la 'drʲapta]

to the left   **la stânga**
[la 'stinga]

Go straight ahead.   **Mergeți drept înainte.**
[merdʒets' drept ina'inte]

Signs

WELCOME!	**BINE AȚI VENIT!**
	[bine 'aʦ/ ve'nit!]
ENTRANCE	**INTRARE**
	[in'trare]
EXIT	**IEȘIRE**
	[je'ʃire]

PUSH	**ÎMPINGEȚI**
	[im'pinʒeʦ/]
PULL	**TRAGEȚI**
	[tra'dʒeʦ/]
OPEN	**DESCHIS**
	[des'kis]
CLOSED	**ÎNCHIS**
	[in'kis]

FOR WOMEN	**PENTRU FEMEI**
	[pentru fe'mej]
FOR MEN	**PENTRU BĂRBAȚI**
	[pentru bər'baʦ/]
GENTLEMEN, GENTS	**BĂRBAȚI**
	[bər'baʦ/]
WOMEN	**FEMEI**
	[fe'mej]

DISCOUNTS	**REDUCERI**
	[re'dutʃer/]
SALE	**OFERTĂ**
	[o'fertə]
FREE	**GRATUIT**
	[gratu'it]
NEW!	**NOU!**
	['nou!]
ATTENTION!	**ATENȚIE!**
	[a'tenʦie!]

NO VACANCIES	**NU MAI SUNT CAMERE DISPONIBILE**
	[nu maj sunt 'kamere dispo'nibile]
RESERVED	**REZERVAT**
	[rezer'vat]
ADMINISTRATION	**CONDUCERE**
	[kon'dutʃere]
STAFF ONLY	**REZERVAT PERSONAL**
	[rezer'vat perso'nal]

BEWARE OF THE DOG!	**ATENȚIE, CÂINE RĂU!** [a'tentsie, 'kɨjne rəu!]
NO SMOKING!	**FUMATUL INTERZIS!** [fu'matul inter'zis!]
DO NOT TOUCH!	**A NU SE ATINGE!** [a nu se a'tinʒe!]
DANGEROUS	**PERICOL** [pe'rikol]
DANGER	**PERICOL GENERAL** [pe'rikol dʒene'ral]
HIGH VOLTAGE	**ATENȚIE ÎNALTĂ TENSIUNE** [a'tentsie ɨnaltə tensi'une]
NO SWIMMING!	**ÎNOTUL INTERZIS!** [i'notul inter'zis!]
OUT OF ORDER	**DEFECT** [de'fekt]
FLAMMABLE	**INFLAMABIL** [infla'mabil]
FORBIDDEN	**INTERZIS** [inter'zis]
NO TRESPASSING!	**ACCES INTERZIS!** [aktʃes inter'zis!]
WET PAINT	**PROASPĂT VOPSIT** [pro'aspət vop'sit]
CLOSED FOR RENOVATIONS	**ÎNCHIS PENTRU RENOVARE** [in'kis 'pentru reno'vare]
WORKS AHEAD	**ATENȚIE SE LUCREAZĂ** [a'tentsie se lu'kriazə]
DETOUR	**TRAFIC DEVIAT** [trafik de'vjat]

Transportation. General phrases

plane	**avion** [a'vjon]
train	**tren** [tren]
bus	**autobuz** [auto'buz]
ferry	**feribot** [feri'bot]
taxi	**taxi** [ta'ksi]
car	**maşină** [ma'ʃinə]

schedule	**orar** [o'rar]
Where can I see the schedule?	**Unde pot vedea orarul?** [unde pot ve'dʲa o'rarul?]
workdays (weekdays)	**zile de lucru** [zile de 'lukru]
weekends	**sfârşit de săptămână** [sfir'ʃit de səptə'minə]
holidays	**sărbători** [sərbəto'ri]

DEPARTURE	**PLECĂRI** [plekərʲ]
ARRIVAL	**SOSIRI** [so'sirʲ]
DELAYED	**ÎNTÂRZIERI** [intirzi'erʲ]
CANCELLED	**ANULĂRI** [anulərʲ]

next (train, etc.)	**următorul** [urmə'torul]
first	**primul** ['primul]
last	**ultimul** ['ultimul]

When is the next ...?	**Când este următorul ...?** [kind 'este urmə'torul ...?]
When is the first ...?	**Când este primul ...?** [kind 'este 'primul ...?]

When is the last ...?

Când este ultimul ...?
[kɨnd 'este 'ultimul ...?]

transfer (change of trains, etc.)

schimb
[skimb]

to make a transfer

a schimba
[a skim'ba]

Do I need to make a transfer?

**Trebuie să schimb ...
(trenul | avionul)?**
[trebuje sə skimb ...
('trenul | a'vjonul)?]

Buying tickets

Where can I buy tickets?	**De unde pot cumpăra bilete?** [de 'unde pot kumpə'ra bi'lete?]
ticket	**bilet** [bi'let]
to buy a ticket	**a cumpăra un bilet** [a kumpə'ra un bi'let]
ticket price	**prețul biletului** [preţsul bi'letului]
Where to?	**În ce direcție?** [ɨn ţʃe di'rektsie?]
To what station?	**La ce stație?** [la ţʃe 'statsie?]
I need ...	**Am nevoie de ...** [am ne'voje de ...]
one ticket	**un bilet** [un bi'let]
two tickets	**două bilete** [dowə bi'lete]
three tickets	**trei bilete** [trej bi'lete]
one-way	**dus** [dus]
round-trip	**dus-întors** [dus-ɨn'tors]
first class	**clasa întâi** [klasa ɨn'tɨj]
second class	**clasa a doua** [klasa a 'dowa]
today	**astăzi** [astəzʲ]
tomorrow	**mâine** [mɨjne]
the day after tomorrow	**poimâine** [po'imɨine]
in the morning	**dimineața** [dimi'nʲatsa]
in the afternoon	**după-masa** ['dupə-'masa]
in the evening	**seara** [sʲara]

aisle seat	**loc la culoar** [lok la kulo'ar]
window seat	**loc la geam** [lok la ʤʲam]
How much?	**Cât costă?** [kɨt 'kostə?]
Can I pay by credit card?	**Pot plăti cu cardul?** [pot plə'ti ku 'kardul?]

Bus

bus	**autobuz** [auto'buz]
intercity bus	**autobuz interurban** [auto'buz interur'ban]
bus stop	**stație de autobuz** [staʦie de auto'buz]
Where's the nearest bus stop?	**Unde este cea mai apropiată stație de autobuz?** [unde 'este ʧa maj apro'pjatə 'staʦie de auto'buz?]
number (bus ~, etc.)	**număr** ['numər]
Which bus do I take to get to ...?	**Ce autobuz trebuie să iau să ajung la ...?** [ʧe auto'buz tre'buje sə jau sə a'ʒun la ...?]
Does this bus go to ...?	**Acest autobuz ajunge la ...?** [a'ʧest auto'buz a'ʒunʒe la ...?]
How frequent are the buses?	**La ce interval vin autobuzele?** [la ʧe inter'val vin auto'buzele?]
every 15 minutes	**la fiecare 15 minute** [la fie'kare 'ʧinʧsprezeʧe mi'nute]
every half hour	**la fiecare jumătate de oră** [la fie'kare ʒumə'tate de 'orə]
every hour	**la fiecare oră** [la fie'kare 'orə]
several times a day	**de câteva ori pe zi** [de kite'va ori pe zi]
... times a day	**de ... ori pe zi** [de ... ori pe zi]
schedule	**orar** [o'rar]
Where can I see the schedule?	**Unde pot vedea orarul?** [unde pot ve'dʲa o'rarul?]
When is the next bus?	**Când este următorul autobuz?** [kind 'este urmə'torul auto'buz?]
When is the first bus?	**Când este primul autobuz?** [kind 'este 'primul auto'buz?]
When is the last bus?	**Când este ultimul autobuz?** [kind 'este 'ultimul auto'buz?]

stop	**stație** [statsie]
next stop	**următoarea stație** [urməto'ar'a 'statsie]
last stop (terminus)	**ultima stație** [ultima 'statsie]
Stop here, please.	**Opriți aici, vă rog.** [o'prits' a'itʃi, və rog]
Excuse me, this is my stop.	**Scuzați-mă, cobor aici.** [sku'zatsi-mə, ko'bor a'itʃi]

Train

train	**tren** [tren]
suburban train	**tren suburban** [tren subur'ban]
long-distance train	**tren pe distanță lungă** [tren pe dis'tanʦə 'lungə]
train station	**o gară** [o 'garə]
Excuse me, where is the exit to the platform?	**Scuzați-mă, unde este ieșirea spre peron?** [sku'zaʦi-mə, 'unde 'este ie'ʃirʲa spre pe'ron?]

Does this train go to ...?	**Acest tren merge la ...?** [a'ʧest tren 'merʤe la ...?]
next train	**următorul tren** [urmə'torul tren]
When is the next train?	**Când este următorul tren?** [kind 'este urmə'torul tren?]
Where can I see the schedule?	**Unde pot vedea mersul trenurilor?** [unde pot ve'dʲa 'mersul 'trenurilor?]
From which platform?	**De la care peron?** [de la kare pe'ron?]
When does the train arrive in ...?	**Când ajunge trenul la ...?** [kind a'ʒunʤe 'trenul la ...?]

Please help me.	**Vă rog să mă ajutați.** [və rog sə mə aʒu'taʦi]
I'm looking for my seat.	**Îmi caut locul.** [imʲ 'kaut 'lokul]
We're looking for our seats.	**Ne căutăm locurile.** [ne kəutəm 'lokurile]

My seat is taken.	**Locul meu este ocupat.** [lokul 'meu 'este oku'pat]
Our seats are taken.	**Locurile noastre sunt ocupate.** [lokurile no'astre sunt oku'pate]
I'm sorry but this is my seat.	**Îmi pare rău dar acesta este locul meu.** [imʲ 'pare rəu dar a'ʧesta 'este 'lokul 'meu]

Is this seat taken? **Este liber acest loc?**
[este 'liber a'tʃest lok?]

May I sit here? **Pot să stau aici?**
[pot sə 'stau a'itʃi?]

On the train. Dialogue (No ticket)

Ticket, please.

Biletul la control.
[bi'letul la kon'trol]

I don't have a ticket.

Nu am bilet.
[nu am bi'let]

I lost my ticket.

Mi-am pierdut biletul.
[mi-am 'pjerdut bi'letul]

I forgot my ticket at home.

Mi-am uitat biletul acasă.
[mi-am 'ujtat bi'letul a'kasə]

You can buy a ticket from me.

Puteți cumpăra un bilet de la mine.
[pu'teʦʲ kumpə'ra un bi'let de la 'mine]

You will also have to pay a fine.

**Va trebui, de asemenea,
să plătiți și o amendă.**
[va 'trebuj, de a'semenʲa,
sə plə'tiʦʲ ʃi o a'mendə]

Okay.

Bine.
['bine]

Where are you going?

Unde mergeți?
[unde mer'ʤeʦi?]

I'm going to ...

Merg la ...
[merg la ...]

How much? I don't understand.

Cât costă? Nu înțeleg.
[kɨt 'kostə? nu ɨnʦe'leg]

Write it down, please.

Scrieți pe ceva, vă rog.
[skri'eʦʲ pe ʧe'va, və rog]

Okay. Can I pay with a credit card?

Bine. Pot plăti cu cardul?
[bine. pot plə'ti ku 'kardul?]

Yes, you can.

Da, puteți.
[da, pu'teʦʲ]

Here's your receipt.

Aceasta este chitanța dumneavoastră.
[a'ʧasta 'este ki'tanʦa dumnʲavo'astrə]

Sorry about the fine.

Îmi pare rău pentru amendă.
[ɨmʲ 'pare rəu 'pentru a'mendə]

That's okay. It was my fault.

Este în regulă. A fost vina mea.
[este ɨn 'regulə. a fost 'vina mʲa]

Enjoy your trip.

Călătorie plăcută!
[kələto'rie plə'kutə!]

Taxi

taxi	**taxi** [ta'ksi]
taxi driver	**şofer de taxi** [ʃo'fer de ta'ksi]
to catch a taxi	**a lua un taxi** [a 'lua un ta'ksi]
taxi stand	**staţie de taxiuri** [sta'ʦie de ta'ksjur']
Where can I get a taxi?	**De unde pot lua un taxi?** [de 'unde pot 'lua un ta'ksi?]
to call a taxi	**a chema un taxi** [a 'kema un ta'ksi]
I need a taxi.	**Am nevoie de un taxi.** [am ne'voje de un ta'ksi]
Right now.	**Acum.** [a'kum]
What is your address (location)?	**Care este adresa dumneavoastră?** [kare 'este a'dresa dumnʲavo'astrə?]
My address is ...	**Adresa mea este ...** [a'dresa mʲa 'este ...]
Your destination?	**Unde mergeţi?** [unde mer'ʤeʦi?]
Excuse me, ...	**Scuzaţi-mă, ...** [sku'zaʦi-mə, ...]
Are you available?	**Sunteţi liber?** [sun'teʦ' 'liber?]
How much is it to get to ...?	**Cât costă până la ...?** [kɨt 'kostə 'pɨnə la ...?]
Do you know where it is?	**Ştiţi unde este?** [ʃtiʦ' 'unde 'este?]
Airport, please.	**La aeroport, vă rog.** [la aero'port, və rog]
Stop here, please.	**Opriţi aici, vă rog.** [o'priʦ' a'iʧi, və rog]
It's not here.	**Nu este aici.** [nu 'este a'iʧi]
This is the wrong address.	**Adresa asta este greşită.** [a'dresa as'ta 'este gre'ʃitə]
Turn left.	**Luaţi-o la stânga.** [lu'aʦi-o la 'stɨnga]
Turn right.	**Luaţi-o la dreapta.** [lu'aʦi-o la 'drʲapta]

How much do I owe you?

Cât vă datorez?
[kit və da'torez?]

I'd like a receipt, please.

Aş dori o chitanţă, vă rog.
[aʃ do'ri o ki'tantsə, və rog]

Keep the change.

Păstraţi restul.
[pəs'tratsʲ 'restul]

Would you please wait for me?

Mă puteţi aştepta, vă rog?
[mə pu'tetsʲ aʃtep'ta, və rog?]

five minutes

cinci minute
[tʃintʃ mi'nute]

ten minutes

zece minute
[zetʃe mi'nute]

fifteen minutes

cincisprezece minute
[tʃintʃisprezetʃe mi'nute]

twenty minutes

douăzeci de minute
[dowə'zetʃi de mi'nute]

half an hour

o jumătate de oră
[o ʒumə'tate de 'orə]

Hotel

Hello.	**Bună ziua.** [bunə 'ziwa]
My name is ...	**Mă numesc ...** [mə nu'mesk ...]
I have a reservation.	**Am o rezervare.** [am o rezer'vare]

I need ...	**Am nevoie de ...** [am ne'voje de ...]
a single room	**o cameră single** [o 'kamerə 'singlə]
a double room	**o cameră dublă** [o 'kamerə 'dublə]
How much is that?	**Cât costă?** [kɨt 'kostə?]
That's a bit expensive.	**Este puțin cam scump.** [este pu'tsin kam skump]

Do you have anything else?	**Mai există alte opțiuni?** [maj e'gzistə 'alte op'tsjuni?]
I'll take it.	**O iau.** [o 'jau]
I'll pay in cash.	**Plătesc în numerar.** [plə'tesk in nume'rar]

I've got a problem.	**Am o problemă.** [am o pro'blemə]
My ... is broken.	**... este stricat /stricată/.** [... 'este stri'kat /stri'katə/]
My ... is out of order.	**... este defect /defectă/.** [... 'este de'fekt /'este de'fektə/]
TV	**Meu televizorul (este stricat)** [meu televi'zorul ('este stri'kat)]
air conditioner	**Aerul meu condiționat (este defect)** [aerul 'meu konditsjo'nat ('este de'fekt)]
tap	**Meu robinetul (este stricat)** [meu robi'netul ('este stri'kat)]

shower	**Meu dușul (este stricat)** [meu 'duʃul ('este stri'kat)]
sink	**Mea chiuveta (este defectă)** [mʲa kju'veta ('este de'fektə)]
safe	**Meu seiful (este stricat)** [meu 'sejful ('este stri'kat)]

door lock	**Încuietoarea (este defectă)** [inkue'toar'a]
electrical outlet	**Mea priza (este defectă)** [m'a 'priza ('este de'fektə)]
hairdryer	**Uscătorul meu de păr (este stricat)** [uskə'torul 'meu de pər ('este stri'kat)]

I don't have ...	**Nu am ...** [nu am ...]
water	**apă** ['apə]
light	**lumină** [lu'minə]
electricity	**curent electric** [ku'rent e'lektric]

Can you give me ...?	**Îmi puteți da ...?** [im' pu'tets' da ...?]
a towel	**un prosop** [un pro'sop]
a blanket	**o pătură** [o 'pəturə]
slippers	**papuci** [pa'putʃi]
a robe	**un halat** [un ha'lat]
shampoo	**nişte şampon** [ʃam'pon]
soap	**nişte săpun** [sə'pun]

I'd like to change rooms.	**Aş dori să îmi schimb camera.** [aʃ do'ri sə imj skimb 'kamera]
I can't find my key.	**Nu îmi găsesc cheia.** [nu imj gə'sesk ke'ja]
Could you open my room, please?	**Puteți să îmi deschideți camera, vă rog?** [pu'tets' sə im' de'skidets' 'kamera, və rog?]

Who's there?	**Cine e?** [tʃine e?]
Come in!	**Intraţi!** [in'trats'!]
Just a minute!	**Un minut!** [un mi'nut!]

Not right now, please.	**Nu acum, vă rog.** [nu a'kum, və rog]
Come to my room, please.	**Veniţi în camera mea, vă rog.** [ve'nits' in 'kamera m'a, və rog]

I'd like to order food service.	**Aş dori să îmi comand de mâncare în cameră.** [aʃ do'ri sə imj ko'mand de min'kare in 'kamerə]
My room number is …	**Numărul camerei mele este …** [numərul 'kamerej mele 'este …]

I'm leaving …	**Plec …** [plek …]
We're leaving …	**Plecăm …** [plekəm …]
right now	**acum** [a'kum]
this afternoon	**în această după-masă** [in a'tʃastə 'dupə-'masə]
tonight	**diseară** [di's'arə]
tomorrow	**mâine** [mijne]
tomorrow morning	**mâine dimineaţă** [mijne dimi'n'atsə]
tomorrow evening	**mâine seară** [mijne 's'arə]
the day after tomorrow	**poimâine** [po'imiine]

I'd like to pay.	**Aş dori să plătesc.** [aʃ do'ri sə plə'tesk]
Everything was wonderful.	**Totul a fost excelent.** [totul a fost ekstʃe'lent]
Where can I get a taxi?	**De unde pot lua un taxi?** [de 'unde pot 'lua un ta'ksi?]
Would you call a taxi for me, please?	**Îmi puteţi chema un taxi, vă rog?** [imj pu'tetsj ke'ma un ta'ksi, və rog?]

Restaurant

Can I look at the menu, please?	**Pot vedea meniul, vă rog?** [pot ve'dʲa me'njul, və rog?]
Table for one.	**O masă pentru o persoană.** [o 'masə 'pentru o perso'anə]
There are two (three, four) of us.	**Suntem două (trei, patru) persoane.** [suntem 'dowə (trej, 'patru) perso'ane]

Smoking	**Fumători** [fumə'tori]
No smoking	**Nefumători** [nefumə'tori]
Excuse me! (addressing a waiter)	**Scuzați-mă!** [sku'zatsi-mə!]
menu	**meniu** [me'nju]
wine list	**lista de vinuri** [lista de 'vinuri]
The menu, please.	**Un meniu, vă rog.** [un me'nju, və rog]

Are you ready to order?	**Sunteți gata să comandați?** [sun'tetsʲ 'gata sə koman'datsʲ?]
What will you have?	**Ce veți servi?** [tʃe 'vetsi ser'vi?]
I'll have ...	**Vreau ...** [vrʲau ...]

I'm a vegetarian.	**Sunt vegetarian.** [sunt vedʒeta'rjan /vedʒeta'rjanə/]
meat	**carne** ['karne]
fish	**pește** ['peʃte]
vegetables	**legume** [le'gume]
Do you have vegetarian dishes?	**Aveți feluri de mâncare vegetariene?** [a'vetsʲ fe'luri de mɨn'kare vedʒe'tariene?]
I don't eat pork.	**Nu mănânc porc.** [nu mə'nɨnk pork]
Band-Aid	**El /Ea/ nu mănâncă carne.** [el /ʲa/ nu mə'nɨnkə 'karne]
I am allergic to ...	**Sunt alergic la ...** [sunt a'lerdʒik /a'lerdʒika/ la ...]

Would you please bring me ...

Vă rog frumos, îmi puteți aduce ...
[və rog fru'mos, ɨmj pu'tetsʲ a'dutʃe ...]

salt | pepper | sugar

sare | piper | zahăr
[sare | pi'per | 'zahər]

coffee | tea | dessert

cafea | ceai | desert
[ka'fʲa | tʃaj | de'sert]

water | sparkling | plain

apă | minerală | plată
[apə | mine'ralə | 'platə]

a spoon | fork | knife

o lingură | o furculiță | un cuțit
[o 'lingurə | o furku'litsə | un ku'tsit]

a plate | napkin

o farfurie | un șervețel
[o farfu'rie | un ʃerve'tsel]

Enjoy your meal!

Poftă bună!
[poftə 'bunə!]

One more, please.

Încă unul /unula/, vă rog.
[ɨnkə 'unul /'unula/, və rog]

It was very delicious.

A fost foarte bun.
[a fost fo'arte bun]

---

check | change | tip

notă | rest | bacșiș
[notə | rest | bak'ʃiʃ]

Check, please.
(Could I have the check, please?)

Nota, vă rog.
[nota, və rog]

Can I pay by credit card?

Pot plăti cu cardul?
[pot plə'ti ku 'kardul?]

I'm sorry, there's a mistake here.

Îmi pare rău, este o greșeală aici.
[ɨmʲ 'pare rəu, 'este o gre'ʃalə a'itʃi]

Shopping

Can I help you?	**Pot să vă ajut?** [pot sə və a'ʒut?]
Do you have ...?	**Aveţi ...?** [a'vetsʲ ...?]
I'm looking for ...	**Caut ...** [kaut ...]
I need ...	**Am nevoie de ...** [am ne'voje de ...]

I'm just looking.	**Doar mă uit.** [do'ar mə uit]
We're just looking.	**Doar ne uităm.** [do'ar ne uitəm]
I'll come back later.	**Mă întorc mai târziu.** [mə ɨn'tork maj tɨr'zju]
We'll come back later.	**Ne întoarcem mai târziu.** [ne ɨnto'artʃem maj tɨr'zju]
discounts | sale	**reduceri | ofertă** [re'dutʃerʲ | o'fertə]

Would you please show me ...	**Îmi puteţi arăta ..., vă rog.** [ɨmʲ pu'tetsʲ arə'ta ..., və rog]
Would you please give me ...	**Îmi puteţi da ..., vă rog.** [ɨmʲ pu'tetsʲ da ..., və rog]
Can I try it on?	**Pot să probez?** [pot sə pro'bez?]
Excuse me, where's the fitting room?	**Nu vă supăraţi, unde este cabina de probă?** [nu və supə'ratsʲ, 'unde 'este ka'bina de 'probə?]
Which color would you like?	**Ce culoare aţi dori?** [tʃe kulo'are 'atsʲ do'ri?]
size | length	**mărime | lungime** [mə'rime | lun'dʒime]
How does it fit?	**Cum vine?** [kum 'vine?]

How much is it?	**Cât costă asta?** [kɨt 'kostə 'asta?]
That's too expensive.	**Este prea scump.** [este prʲa skump]
I'll take it.	**Îl iau /O iau/.** [ɨl 'jau /o 'jau/]

Excuse me, where do I pay?	**Nu vă supărați, unde plătesc?** [nu və supə'rаts', 'unde plə'tesk?]
Will you pay in cash or credit card?	**Plătiți în numerar sau cu cardul?** [plə'tits' in nume'rar sau ku 'kardul?]
In cash | with credit card	**În numerar | cu cardul** [in nume'rar | ku 'kardul]

Do you want the receipt?	**Doriți chitanță?** [do'rits' ki'tantsə?]
Yes, please.	**Da, vă rog.** [da, və rog]
No, it's OK.	**Nu, este în regulă.** [nu, 'este in 'regulə]
Thank you. Have a nice day!	**Mulțumesc. O zi bună!** [multsu'mesk. o zi 'bunə!]

In town

Excuse me, ...	**Îmi cer scuze.** [im^j t͡ʃer 'skuze]
I'm looking for ...	**Caut ...** [kaut ...]
the subway	**metroul** [me'troul]
my hotel	**hotelul** [ho'telul]
the movie theater	**cinematograful** [t͡ʃinemato'graful]
a taxi stand	**o stație de taxi** [o 'stat͡sie de ta'ksi]

an ATM	**un bancomat** [un banko'mat]
a foreign exchange office	**un birou de schimb valutar** [un bi'rou de skimb valu'tar]
an internet café	**un internet café** [un inter'net kafé]
... street	**... strada** [... 'strada]
this place	**locul acesta** [lokul a't͡ʃesta]

Do you know where ... is?	**Știți unde este ...?** [ʃtit͡s^j 'unde 'este ...?]
Which street is this?	**Ce stradă este aceasta?** [t͡ʃe 'stradə 'este a't͡ʃasta?]
Show me where we are right now.	**Arătați-mi unde ne aflăm acum.** [arə'tat͡si-mi 'unde ne afləm a'kum]
Can I get there on foot?	**Pot ajunge acolo pe jos?** [pot a'ʒunʒe a'kolo pe ʒos?]
Do you have a map of the city?	**Aveți o hartă a orașului?** [a'vet͡s^j o 'hartə a ora'ʃului?]

How much is a ticket to get in?	**Cât costă un bilet de intrare?** [kit 'kostə un bi'let de in'trare?]
Can I take pictures here?	**Este permis fotografiatul aici?** [este per'mis fotogra'fjatul a'it͡ʃi?]
Are you open?	**Este deschis?** [este des'kis?]

When do you open?	**La ce oră deschideți?**
	[la tʃe 'orə des'kidetsʲ?]
When do you close?	**La ce oră închideți?**
	[la tʃe 'orə in'kidetsʲ?]

Money

money	**bani** ['bani]
cash	**numerar** [nume'rar]
paper money	**bancnote** [bank'note]
loose change	**mărunţiş** [mərun'tsiʃ]
check | change | tip	**notă | rest | bacşiş** [notə | rest | bak'ʃiʃ]
credit card	**card bancar** [kard ban'kar]
wallet	**portofel** [porto'fel]
to buy	**a cumpăra** [a kumpə'ra]
to pay	**a plăti** [a plə'ti]
fine	**amendă** [a'mendə]
free	**gratis** [gratis]
Where can I buy ...?	**De unde pot cumpăra ...?** [de 'unde pot kumpə'ra ...?]
Is the bank open now?	**Banca este deschisă acum?** [banka 'este des'kisə a'kum?]
When does it open?	**Când deschide?** [kind des'kide?]
When does it close?	**Când închide?** [kind in'kide?]
How much?	**Cât costă?** [kit 'kostə?]
How much is this?	**Cât costă asta?** [kit 'kostə 'asta?]
That's too expensive.	**Este prea scump.** [este pr'a skump]
Excuse me, where do I pay?	**Nu vă supăraţi, unde plătesc?** [nu və supə'ratsʲ, 'unde plə'tesk?]
Check, please.	**Nota, vă rog.** [nota, və rog]

Can I pay by credit card?

Pot plăti cu cardul?
[pot plə'ti ku 'kardul?]

Is there an ATM here?

Există vreun bancomat aici?
[e'gzistə 'vreun banko'mat a'itʃi?]

I'm looking for an ATM.

Caut un bancomat.
[kaut un banko'mat]

I'm looking for a foreign exchange office.

Caut un birou de schimb valutar.
[kaut un bi'rou de skimb valu'tar]

I'd like to change ...

Aş dori să schimb ...
[aʃ do'ri sə skimb ...]

What is the exchange rate?

Care este cursul de schimb?
[kare 'este 'kursul de skimb?]

Do you need my passport?

Vă trebuie paşaportul meu?
[və 'trebuje paʃa'portul 'meu?]

Time

What time is it?	**Cât este ceasul?** [kɨt 'este 'tʃasul?]
When?	**Când?** [kɨnd?]
At what time?	**La ce oră?** [la tʃe 'orə?]
now | later | after …	**acum | mai târziu | după …** [a'kum | maj tɨr'zju | 'dupə …]

one o'clock	**ora unu** [ora 'unu]
one fifteen	**unu şi un sfert** [unu ʃi un sfert]
one thirty	**unu şi jumătate** [unu ʃi ʒumə'tate]
one forty-five	**unu patruzeci şi cinci** [unu patru'zetʃ ʃi 'tʃintʃ]

one | two | three	**unu | două | trei** [unu | 'dowə | trej]
four | five | six	**patru | cinci | şase** [patru | 'tʃintʃ | 'ʃase]
seven | eight | nine	**şapte | opt | nouă** [ʃapte | opt | 'nowə]
ten | eleven | twelve	**zece | unsprezece | doisprezece** [zetʃe | 'unsprezetʃe | 'dojsprezetʃe]

in …	**în …** [ɨn …]
five minutes	**cinci minute** [tʃintʃ mi'nute]
ten minutes	**zece minute** [zetʃe mi'nute]
fifteen minutes	**cincisprezece minute** [tʃintʃisprezetʃe mi'nute]
twenty minutes	**douăzeci de minute** [dowə'zetʃi de mi'nute]
half an hour	**într-o jumătate de oră** [ɨntr-o ʒumə'tate de 'orə]
an hour	**într-o oră** [ɨntr-o 'orə]

in the morning	**dimineața** [dimi'nʲatsa]
early in the morning	**dimineața devreme** [dimi'nʲatsa de'vreme]
this morning	**dimineața aceasta** [dimi'nʲatsa a'tʃasta]
tomorrow morning	**mâine dimineață** [mɨjne dimi'nʲatsə]

in the middle of the day	**la prânz** [la prinz]
in the afternoon	**după-masa** ['dupə-'masa]
in the evening	**seara** [sʲara]
tonight	**diseară** [di'sʲarə]

at night	**noaptea** [no'aptʲa]
yesterday	**ieri** [jerʲ]
today	**azi** [azʲ]
tomorrow	**mâine** [mɨjne]
the day after tomorrow	**poimâine** [po'imɨine]

What day is it today?	**Ce zi este astăzi?** [tʃe zi 'este astəzʲ?]
It's ...	**Azi este ...** [azʲ 'este ...]
Monday	**Luni** [lunʲ]
Tuesday	**Marți** [martsʲ]
Wednesday	**Miercuri** [mjerkurʲ]

Thursday	**Joi** [ʒoj]
Friday	**Vineri** [vinerʲ]
Saturday	**Sâmbătă** [simbətə]
Sunday	**Duminică** [du'minikə]

Greetings. Introductions

Hello.
Bună ziua.
[bunə 'ziwa]

Pleased to meet you.
Îmi pare bine.
[im^j 'pare 'bine]

Me too.
Şi mie.
[ʃi 'mie]

I'd like you to meet ...
Aş vrea să vă fac cunoştinţă cu ...
[aʃ 'vr^ja sə və fak kunoʃ'tintsə ku ...]

Nice to meet you.
Mă bucur de cunoştinţă.
[mə bukur de kunoʃ'tintsə]

How are you?
Ce mai faceţi?
[tʃe maj 'fatʃets^j?]

My name is ...
Mă numesc ...
[mə nu'mesk ...]

His name is ...
El este ...
[el 'este ...]

Her name is ...
Ea este ...
[ʲa 'este ...]

What's your name?
Cum vă numiţi?
[kum və nu'mits^j?]

What's his name?
Cum se numeşte dumnealui?
[kum se nu'meʃte dum'nalui?]

What's her name?
Cum se numeşte dumneaei?
[kum se nu'meʃte dumna'ej?]

What's your last name?
Care este numele dumneavoastră de familie?
[kare 'este 'numele dumn^javo'astrə de fa'milie?]

You can call me ...
Îmi puteţi spune ...
[im^j pu'tets^j 'spune ...]

Where are you from?
De unde sunteţi?
[de 'unde 'suntets^j?]

I'm from ...
Sunt din ...
[sunt din ...]

What do you do for a living?
Cu ce vă ocupaţi?
[ku tʃe və oku'pats^j?]

Who is this?
Cine este acesta /aceasta/?
[tʃine 'este a'tʃesta /a'tʃasta/?]

Who is he?
Cine este el?
[tʃine 'este el?]

Who is she?	**Cine este ea?**
	[ʧine 'este ja?]
Who are they?	**Cine sunt ei /ele/?**
	[ʧine sunt ej /'ele/?]

This is ...	**Acesta /Aceasta/ este ...**
	[a'ʧesta /a'ʧasta/ 'este ...]
my friend (masc.)	**prietenul meu**
	[pri'etenul 'meu]
my friend (fem.)	**prietena mea**
	[pri'etena mʲa]
my husband	**soțul meu**
	[soʦul 'meu]
my wife	**soția mea**
	[so'ʦia mʲa]

my father	**tatăl meu**
	[tatəl 'meu]
my mother	**mama mea**
	[mama mʲa]
my brother	**fratele meu**
	[fratele 'meu]
my sister	**sora mea**
	[sora mʲa]
my son	**fiul meu**
	[fjul 'meu]
my daughter	**fiica mea**
	[fiika mʲa]

This is our son.	**Acesta este fiul nostru.**
	[a'ʧesta 'este fjul 'nostru]
This is our daughter.	**Aceasta este fiica noastră.**
	[a'ʧasta 'este 'fiika no'astrə]
These are my children.	**Aceștia sunt copiii mei.**
	[a'ʧeʃtja sunt ko'piij mej]
These are our children.	**Aceștia sunt copiii noștri.**
	[a'ʧeʃtja sunt ko'piij 'noʃtri]

Farewells

Good bye!	**Le revedere!** [le reve'dere!]
Bye! (inform.)	**Pa!** [pa!]
See you tomorrow.	**Pe mâine.** [pe 'miine]
See you soon.	**Pe curând.** [pe ku'rind]
See you at seven.	**Ne vedem la şapte.** [ne ve'dem la 'ʃapte]
Have fun!	**Distracţie plăcută!** [dis'traktsie plə'kutə!]
Talk to you later.	**Ne auzim mai târziu.** [ne au'zim maj tir'zju]
Have a nice weekend.	**Week-end plăcut.** [wi'kend plə'kut]
Good night.	**Noapte bună.** [no'apte 'bunə]
It's time for me to go.	**E timpul să mă retrag.** [e 'timpul sə mə re'trag]
I have to go.	**Trebuie să plec.** [trebuje sə plek]
I will be right back.	**Revin imediat.** [re'vin ime'djat]
It's late.	**Este târziu.** [este tir'zju]
I have to get up early.	**Trebuie să mă trezesc devreme.** [trebuje sə mə tre'zesk de'vreme]
I'm leaving tomorrow.	**Plec mâine.** [plek 'miine]
We're leaving tomorrow.	**Plecăm mâine.** [plekəm 'miine]
Have a nice trip!	**Călătorie plăcută!** [kələto'rie plə'kutə!]
It was nice meeting you.	**Mi-a părut bine de cunoştinţă.** [mia pə'rut 'bine de kunoʃ'tintsə]
It was nice talking to you.	**Mi-a părut bine să stăm de vorbă.** [mia pə'rut 'bine sə stəm de 'vorbə]
Thanks for everything.	**Vă mulţumesc pentru tot.** [və mulʦu'mesk 'pentru tot]

I had a very good time.

M-am simțit foarte bine.
[mam sim'ţsit fo'arte 'bine]

We had a very good time.

Ne-am simțit foarte bine.
[ne-am sim'ţsit fo'arte 'bine]

It was really great.

A fost minunat.
[a fost minu'nat]

I'm going to miss you.

O să îți simt lipsa.
[o sə 'iţsʲ simt 'lipsa]

We're going to miss you.

Îți vom simți lipsa.
[iţsʲ vom 'simţsʲ 'lipsa]

Good luck!

Noroc!
[no'rok!]

Say hi to ...

Salută-l pe... /Salut-o pe .../
[sa'lutəl pe... /sa'luto pe .../]

Foreign language

I don't understand.	**Nu înțeleg.** [nu intse'leg]
Write it down, please.	**Scrieți pe ceva, vă rog.** [skri'etsʲ pe tʃe'va, və rog]
Do you speak ...?	**Vorbiți ...?** [vor'bitsʲ ...?]

I speak a little bit of ...	**Vorbesc puțină ...** [vor'besk pu'tsinə ...]
English	**engleză** [en'glezə]
Turkish	**turcă** ['turkə]
Arabic	**arabă** [a'rabə]
French	**franceză** [fran'tʃezə]

German	**germană** [dʒer'manə]
Italian	**italiană** [itali'anə]
Spanish	**spaniolă** [spa'njolə]
Portuguese	**portugheză** [portu'gezə]
Chinese	**chineză** [ki'nezə]
Japanese	**japoneză** [ʒapo'nezə]

Can you repeat that, please.	**Vă rog să repetați.** [və rog sə repe'tatsʲ]
I understand.	**Am înțeles.** [am intse'les]
I don't understand.	**Nu înțeleg.** [nu intse'leg]
Please speak more slowly.	**Vă rog să vorbiți mai rar.** [və rog sə vor'bitsʲ maj rar]

Is that correct? (Am I saying it right?)	**Așa se spune?** [a'ʃa se 'spune?]
What is this? (What does this mean?)	**Ce e asta?** [tʃe e 'asta?]

Apologies

Excuse me, please.	**Îmi cer scuze.** [imʲ tʃer 'skuze]
I'm sorry.	**Îmi pare rău.** [imʲ 'pare rəu]
I'm really sorry.	**Îmi pare foarte rău.** [imʲ 'pare fo'arte rəu]
Sorry, it's my fault.	**Scuze, este vina mea.** [skuze, 'este 'vina mʲa]
My mistake.	**Am greşit.** [am gre'ʃit]
May I ...?	**Aş putea ...?** [aʃ pu'tʲa ...?]
Do you mind if I ...?	**Vă deranjează dacă ...?** [və deran'ʒʲazə 'dakə ...?]
It's OK.	**Nu face nimic.** [nu 'fatʃe ni'mik]
It's all right.	**Este în regulă.** [este in 'regulə]
Don't worry about it.	**Nu aveţi pentru ce.** [nu a'vetsʲ 'pentru tʃe]

Agreement

Yes.	**Da.** [da]
Yes, sure.	**Da, desigur.** [da, de'sigur]
OK (Good!)	**Bine!** ['bine!]
Very well.	**Foarte bine.** [fo'arte 'bine]
Certainly!	**Cu siguranţă!** [ku sigu'rantsə!]
I agree.	**Sunt de acord.** [sunt de a'kord]
That's correct.	**Corect.** [ko'rekt]
That's right.	**Aşa e.** [a'ʃa e]
You're right.	**Ai dreptate.** [aj drep'tate]
I don't mind.	**Nu mă deranjează.** [nu mə deran'ʒʲazə]
Absolutely right.	**Fix aşa.** [fiks aʃa]
It's possible.	**Poate.** [po'ate]
That's a good idea.	**E o idee bună.** [e o i'dee 'bunə]
I can't say no.	**Nu pot să refuz.** [nu pot sə re'fuz]
I'd be happy to.	**Mi-ar face plăcere.** [mi-ar 'fatʃe plə'tʃere]
With pleasure.	**Cu plăcere.** [ku plə'tʃere]

Refusal. Expressing doubt

No.
Nu.
[nu]

Certainly not.
Cu siguranţă nu.
[ku sigu'ranțə nu]

I don't agree.
Nu sunt de acord.
[nu sunt de a'kord]

I don't think so.
Nu cred.
[nu kred]

It's not true.
Nu e adevărat.
[nu e adevə'rat]

You are wrong.
Vă înşelaţi.
[və înʃe'lațʲ]

I think you are wrong.
Cred că faceţi o greşeală.
[kred ʧə 'fatʃeʦʲ o gre'ʃʲalə]

I'm not sure.
Nu sunt sigur.
[nu sunt si'gur /si'gurə/]

It's impossible.
Este imposibil.
[este impo'sibil]

Nothing of the kind (sort)!
Nici vorbă!
[niʧi 'vorbə!]

The exact opposite.
Exact pe dos.
[e'gzakt pe dos]

I'm against it.
Sunt împotrivă.
[sunt împo'trivə]

I don't care.
Nu-mi pasă.
[nu-mi 'pasə]

I have no idea.
Nu am idee.
[nu am i'dee]

I doubt it.
Mă cam îndoiesc.
[mə kam îndo'jesk]

Sorry, I can't.
Îmi pare rău, nu pot.
[îmʲ 'pare rəu, nu pot]

Sorry, I don't want to.
Îmi pare rău, nu vreau.
[îmʲ 'pare rəu, nu 'vrʲau]

Thank you, but I don't need this.
Mulţumesc dar nu am nevoie.
[mulțsu'mesk dar nu am ne'voje]

It's getting late.
Se face târziu.
[se 'fatʃe tîr'zju]

I have to get up early.	**Trebuie să mă trezesc devreme.** [trebuje sə mə tre'zesk de'vreme]
I don't feel well.	**Nu mă simt bine.** [nu mə simt 'bine]

Expressing gratitude

Thank you.
Mulțumesc.
[mulʦu'mesk]

Thank you very much.
Vă mulțumesc foarte mult.
[və mulʦu'mesk fo'arte mult]

I really appreciate it.
Mulțumesc frumos.
[mulʦu'mesk fru'mos /frumo'asə/]

I'm really grateful to you.
Vă sunt recunoscător /recunoscătoare/.
[və sunt rekunoskə'tor /rekunoskəto'are/]

We are really grateful to you.
Vă suntem recunoscători.
[və 'suntem rekunoskə'tori]

Thank you for your time.
Vă mulțumesc pentru timpul acordat.
[və mulʦu'mesk 'pentru 'timpul akor'dat]

Thanks for everything.
Mulțumesc pentru tot.
[mulʦu'mesk 'pentru tot]

Thank you for ...
Mulțumesc pentru ...
[mulʦu'mesk 'pentru ...]

your help
ajutor
[aʒu'tor]

a nice time
timpul petrecut împreună
[timpul petre'kut imprə'unə]

a wonderful meal
o masă excelentă
[o 'masə eksʧe'lentə]

a pleasant evening
o seară plăcută
[o 'sʲarə plə'kutə]

a wonderful day
o zi minunată
[o zi minu'natə]

an amazing journey
o călătorie extraordinară
[o kələto'rie ekstraordi'narə]

Don't mention it.
Nu aveți pentru ce.
[nu a'veʦʲ 'pentru ʧe]

You are welcome.
Cu plăcere.
[ku plə'ʧere]

Any time.
Oricând.
[ori'kɨnd]

My pleasure.
Plăcerea este de partea mea.
[plə'ʧerʲa 'este de 'partʲa mʲa]

Forget it.

N-ai pentru ce.
[naj 'pentru t͡ʃe]

Don't worry about it.

Pentru puțin.
[pentru put'sin]

Congratulations. Best wishes

Congratulations!

Felicitări!
[feliʧi'tɛri!]

Happy birthday!

La mulţi ani!
[la 'mulʦi anʲ!]

Merry Christmas!

Crăciun fericit!
[krə'ʧiun feri'ʧit!]

Happy New Year!

Un An Nou fericit!
[un an nou feri'ʧit!]

Happy Easter!

Paşte fericit!
[paʃte feri'ʧit!]

Happy Hanukkah!

Hanuka fericită!
[hanuka feri'ʧitə!]

I'd like to propose a toast.

Aş dori să închin în toast.
[aʃ do'ri sə in'kin in tost]

Cheers!

Noroc!
[no'rok!]

Let's drink to ...!

Să bem pentru ...!
[sə bem 'pentru ...!]

To our success!

Pentru succesul nostru!
[pentru suk'ʧesul 'nostru!]

To your success!

Pentru succesul dumneavoastră!
[pentru suk'ʧesul dumnʲavo'astrə!]

Good luck!

Baftă!
['baftə!]

Have a nice day!

Să aveţi o zi frumoasă!
[sə a'veʦi o zi frumo'asə!]

Have a good holiday!

Vacanţă plăcută!
[va'kanʦə plə'kutə!]

Have a safe journey!

Drum bun!
[drum bun!]

I hope you get better soon!

Multă sănătate!
[multə sənə'tate!]

Socializing

Why are you sad?	**De ce eşti supărat /supărată/?** [de ʧe 'eʃtʲ supə'rat /supə'ratə/?]
Smile! Cheer up!	**Zâmbeşte!** [zɨm'beʃte!]
Are you free tonight?	**Eşti liber /liberă/ în seara asta?** [eʃtʲ 'liber /'liberə/ ɨn 'sʲara 'asta?]

May I offer you a drink?	**Pot să îţi fac cinste cu o băutură?** [pot sə 'iʦʲ fak 'ʧinste ku o bəu'turə?]
Would you like to dance?	**Vrei să dansezi?** [vrej sə dan'sezi?]
Let's go to the movies.	**Hai să mergem la film.** [haj sə 'merdʒem la film]

May I invite you to ...?	**Pot să te invit la ...?** [pot sə te in'vit la ...?]
a restaurant	**un restaurant** [un restau'rant]
the movies	**film** [film]
the theater	**teatru** [te'atru]
go for a walk	**o plimbare** [o plim'bare]

At what time?	**La ce oră?** [la ʧe 'orə?]
tonight	**diseară** [di'sʲarə]
at six	**la şase** [la 'ʃase]
at seven	**la şapte** [la 'ʃapte]
at eight	**la opt** [la opt]
at nine	**la nouă** [la 'nowə]

Do you like it here?	**Îţi place aici?** [iʦʲ 'plaʧie a'iʧi?]
Are you here with someone?	**Eşti cu cineva?** [eʃtʲ ku ʧine'va?]
I'm with my friend.	**Sunt cu un prieten /o prietenă/.** [sunt ku un pri'eten /o pri'etenə/]

I'm with my friends.	**Sunt cu niște prieteni.** [sunt ku 'niʃte pri'etenj]
No, I'm alone.	**Nu, sunt singur /singură/.** [nu, sunt 'singur /'singurə/]

Do you have a boyfriend?	**Ai prieten?** [aj pri'eten?]
I have a boyfriend.	**Am prieten.** [am pri'eten]
Do you have a girlfriend?	**Ai prietenă?** [aj pri'etenə?]
I have a girlfriend.	**Am prietenă.** [am pri'etenə]

Can I see you again?	**Pot să te mai văd?** [pot sə te maj vəd?]
Can I call you?	**Pot să te sun?** [pot sə te sun?]
Call me. (Give me a call.)	**Sună-mă.** ['sunə-mə]
What's your number?	**Care este numărul tău de telefon?** [kare 'este 'numərul təu de tele'fon?]
I miss you.	**Mi-e dor de tine.** [mi-e dor de 'tine]

You have a beautiful name.	**Ce nume frumos ai.** [tʃe 'nume 'frumos aj]
I love you.	**Te iubesc.** [te ju'besk]
Will you marry me?	**Vrei să fii soția mea?** [vrej sə fii sot'sia mʲa?]
You're kidding!	**Glumești!** [glu'meʃti!]
I'm just kidding.	**Glumeam.** [glu'mʲam]

Are you serious?	**Vorbiți serios?** [vor'bitsʲ se'rjos?]
I'm serious.	**Vorbesc serios.** [vor'besk se'rjos]
Really?!	**Serios?!** [se'rjos?!]
It's unbelievable!	**Incredibil!** [inkre'dibil!]
I don't believe you.	**Nu vă cred.** [nu və kred]
I can't.	**Nu pot.** [nu pot]
I don't know.	**Nu știu.** [nu 'ʃtiu]
I don't understand you.	**Nu vă înțeleg.** [nu və intse'leg]

Please go away.	**Vă rog să plecați.** [və rog sə ple'katsʲ]
Leave me alone!	**Lăsați-mă în pace!** [lə'satsi-mə ɨn 'patʃe!]

I can't stand him.	**Nu pot să îl sufăr.** [nu pot sə ɨl 'sufər]
You are disgusting!	**Sunteți enervant!** [sun'tetsʲ ener'vant!]
I'll call the police!	**Chem poliția!** [kem po'litsja!]

Sharing impressions. Emotions

I like it.	**Îmi place.** [imʲ 'platʃe]
Very nice.	**Foarte drăguţ.** [fo'arte dre'guts]
That's great!	**Minunat!** [minu'nat!]
It's not bad.	**Nu e rău.** [nu e rəu]

I don't like it.	**Nu îmi place.** [nu imj 'platʃe]
It's not good.	**Nu e bine.** [nu e 'bine]
It's bad.	**E grav.** [e grav]
It's very bad.	**E foarte grav.** [e fo'arte grav]
It's disgusting.	**E dezgustător.** [e dezgustə'tor]

I'm happy.	**Sunt fericit /fericită/.** [sunt feri'tʃit /feri'tʃitə/]
I'm content.	**Sunt mulţumit /mulţumită/.** [sunt multsu'mit /multsu'mitə/]
I'm in love.	**Sunt îndrăgostit /îndrăgostită/.** [sunt indrəgos'tit /indrəgos'titə/]
I'm calm.	**Sunt calm /calmă/.** [sunt kalm /'kalmə/]
I'm bored.	**Mă plictisesc.** [mə plikti'sesk]

I'm tired.	**Sunt obosit /obosită/.** [sunt obo'sit /obo'sitə/]
I'm sad.	**Sunt trist /tristă/.** [sunt trist /'tristə/]
I'm frightened.	**Mi-e frică.** [mi-e 'frikə]

I'm angry.	**Sunt nervos /nervoasă/.** [sunt ner'vos /nervo'asə/]
I'm worried.	**Sunt îngrijorat /îngrijorată/.** [sunt ingriʒo'rat /ingriʒo'ratə/]
I'm nervous.	**Sunt neliniştit /neliniştită/.** [sunt neliniʃ'tit /neliniʃ'titə/]

I'm jealous. (envious)	**Sunt gelos /geloasă/.** [sunt ʤe'los /ʤelo'asə/]
I'm surprised.	**Sunt surprins /surprinsă/.** [sunt sur'prins /sur'prinsə/]
I'm perplexed.	**Sunt nedumerit /nedumerită/.** [sunt nedume'rit /nedume'ritə/]

Problems. Accidents

I've got a problem.
Am o problemă.
[am o pro'blemə]

We've got a problem.
Avem o problemă.
[a'vem o pro'blemə]

I'm lost.
M-am rătăcit.
[mam rətə'tʃit]

I missed the last bus (train).
Am pierdut ultimul autobuz (tren).
[am 'pjerdut 'ultimul auto'buz (tren)]

I don't have any money left.
Am rămas fără niciun ban.
[am rə'mas 'fərə 'nitʃiun ban]

I've lost my ...
Mi-am pierdut ...
[mi-am 'pjerdut ...]

Someone stole my ...
Cineva mi-a furat ...
[tʃine'va mi-a fu'rat ...]

passport
paşaportul
[paʃa'portul]

wallet
portofelul
[porto'felul]

papers
actele
['aktele]

ticket
biletul
[bi'letul]

money
banii
['banii]

handbag
geanta
[dʒanta]

camera
aparat (n) foto
[apa'rat 'foto]

laptop
laptopul
[ləp'topul]

tablet computer
tableta
[tab'leta]

mobile phone
telefonul mobil
[tele'fonul mo'bil]

Help me!
Ajutaţi-mă!
[aʒu'tatsi-mə!]

What's happened?
Ce s-a întâmplat?
[tʃe sa intim'plat?]

fire
incendiu
[in'tʃendju]

shooting	împuşcături
	[împuʃkə'turi]
murder	crimă
	['krimə]
explosion	explozie
	[eks'plozie]
fight	luptă
	['luptə]

Call the police!	Chemați poliția!
	[ke'matsʲ po'liʦja!]
Please hurry up!	Grabiți-vă, vă rog!
	[gra'biʦi-və, və rog!]
I'm looking for the police station.	Caut secția de poliție.
	[kaut 'sekʦja de po'liʦje]
I need to make a call.	Trebuie să dau un telefon.
	[trebuje sə dau un tele'fon]
May I use your phone?	Pot folosi telefonul dumneavoastră?
	[pot folo'si tele'fonul dumnʲavo'astrə?]

I've been ...	Am fost ...
	[am fost ...]
mugged	tâlhărit /tâlhărită/
	[tɨlhə'rit /tɨlhə'ritə/]
robbed	jefuit /jefuită/
	[ʒefu'it /ʒefu'itə/]
raped	violată
	[vio'latə]
attacked (beaten up)	atacat /atacată/
	[ata'kat /ata'katə/]

Are you all right?	Sunteți bine?
	[sun'tetsʲ 'bine?]
Did you see who it was?	Ați văzut cine era?
	[atsʲ və'zut ʧine e'ra?]
Would you be able to recognize the person?	Ați fi în stare să recunoașteți făptaşul?
	[atsʲ fi ɨn 'stare sə re'kunoaʃteʦi fəpta'ʃul?]
Are you sure?	Sunteți sigur /sigură/?
	[sun'tetsʲ 'sigur /'sigurə/?]

Please calm down.	Vă rog să vă calmați.
	[və rog sə və kal'matsʲ]
Take it easy!	Liniștiți-vă!
	[liniʃtiʦi-və!]
Don't worry!	Nu vă faceți griji!
	[nu və 'fatʃetsʲ griʒʲ!]
Everything will be fine.	Totul va fi bine.
	[totul va fi 'bine]
Everything's all right.	Totul este în regulă.
	[totul 'este ɨn 'regulə]

Come here, please.	**Veniți aici, vă rog.** [ve'nitsi a'itʃi, və rog]
I have some questions for you.	**Am câteva întrebări pentru dumneavoastră.** [am kite'va intre'bɛrj 'pentru dumnʲavo'astrə]
Wait a moment, please.	**Așteptați o clipă, vă rog.** [aʃtep'tatsʲ o 'klipə, və rog]
Do you have any I.D.?	**Aveți vreun act de identitate?** [a'vetsʲ 'vreun akt de identi'tate?]
Thanks. You can leave now.	**Mulțumesc. Puteți pleca acum.** [mulʦu'mesk. Pu'tetsʲ ple'ka a'kum]
Hands behind your head!	**Mâinile la ceafă!** [mijnile la 'tʃafə!]
You're under arrest!	**Sunteți arestat /arestată/!** [sun'tetsʲ ares'tat /ares'tatə/!]

Health problems

Please help me.	**Vă rog să mă ajutați.** [və rog sə mə aʒu'tatsʲ]
I don't feel well.	**Mi-e rău.** [mi-e 'rəu]
My husband doesn't feel well.	**Soțului meu îi este rău.** [sotsului 'meu ɨi 'este rəu]
My son ...	**Fiului meu ...** [fjului 'meu ...]
My father ...	**Tatălui meu ...** [tatəlui 'meu ...]
My wife doesn't feel well.	**Soției mele îi este rău.** [so'tsiej 'mele ɨi 'este rəu]
My daughter ...	**Fiicei mele ...** [fiitʃej 'mele ...]
My mother ...	**Mamei mele ...** [mamej 'mele ...]
I've got a ...	**Mă doare ...** [mə do'are ...]
headache	**capul** ['kapul]
sore throat	**în gât** [ɨn gɨt]
stomach ache	**stomacul** [sto'makul]
toothache	**o măsea** [o mə'sʲa]
I feel dizzy.	**Sunt amețit /amețită/.** [sunt ame'tsit /ame'tsitə/]
He has a fever.	**El are febră.** [el are 'febrə]
She has a fever.	**Ea are febră.** [ja are 'febrə]
I can't breathe.	**Nu pot să respir.** [nu pot sə res'pir]
I'm short of breath.	**Respir greu.** [res'pir 'greu]
I am asthmatic.	**Am astm.** [am astm]
I am diabetic.	**Am diabet.** [am dia'bet]

I can't sleep.	**Nu pot să form.** [nu pot sə form]
food poisoning	**intoxicație alimentară** [intoksi'katsie alimen'tarə]

It hurts here.	**Mă doare aici.** [mə do'are a'itʃi]
Help me!	**Ajutor!** [aʒu'tor!]
I am here!	**Sunt aici!** [sunt a'itʃi!]
We are here!	**Suntem aici!** [suntem a'itʃi!]
Get me out of here!	**Scoateți-mă de aici!** [skoa'tetsi-mə de a'itʃi!]
I need a doctor.	**Am nevoie de un doctor.** [am ne'voje de un dok'tor]
I can't move.	**Nu pot să mă mișc.** [nu pot sə mə miʃk]
I can't move my legs.	**Nu îmi pot mișca picioarele.** [nu imj pot 'miʃka pitʃio'arele]

I have a wound.	**Sunt rănit /rănită/.** [sunt rə'nit /rə'nitə/]
Is it serious?	**Este grav?** [este grav?]
My documents are in my pocket.	**Actele mele sunt în buzunar.** [aktele 'mele sunt in buzu'nar]
Calm down!	**Calmați-vă!** [kal'matsi-və!]
May I use your phone?	**Pot folosi telefonul dumneavoastră?** [pot folo'si tele'fonul dumn'avo'astrə?]

Call an ambulance!	**Chemați o ambulanță!** [ke'matsj o ambu'lantsə!]
It's urgent!	**Este urgent!** [este ur'dʒent!]
It's an emergency!	**Este o urgență!** [este o ur'dʒentsə!]
Please hurry up!	**Grabiți-vă, vă rog!** [gra'bitsi-və, və rog!]
Would you please call a doctor?	**Vreți să chemați un doctor?** [vretsj sə ke'matsj un 'doktor?]
Where is the hospital?	**Unde este spitalul?** [unde 'este spi'talul?]

How are you feeling?	**Cum vă simțiți?** [kum və sim'tsitsj?]
Are you all right?	**Sunteți bine?** [sun'tetsj 'bine?]
What's happened?	**Ce s-a întâmplat?** [tʃe sa intim'plat?]

I feel better now.

Mă simt mai bine acum.
[mə simt maj 'bine a'kum]

It's OK.

E bine.
[e 'bine]

It's all right.

E în regulă.
[e in 'regulə]

At the pharmacy

pharmacy (drugstore)	**farmacie** [farma'ʧie]
24-hour pharmacy	**farmacie non-stop** [farma'ʧie non-stop]
Where is the closest pharmacy?	**Unde este cea mai apropiată farmacie?** [unde 'este ʧa maj apro'pjatə farma'ʧie?]

Is it open now?	**Este deschis acum?** [este des'kis a'kum?]
At what time does it open?	**La ce oră deschide?** [la ʧe 'orə des'kide?]
At what time does it close?	**La ce oră închide?** [la ʧe 'orə in'kide?]

Is it far?	**Este departe?** [este de'parte?]
Can I get there on foot?	**Pot merge pe jos până acolo?** [pot 'merʤe pe ʒos 'pinə a'kolo?]
Can you show me on the map?	**Îmi puteți arăta pe hartă?** [imʲ pu'teʦʲ arə'ta pe 'hartə?]

Please give me something for …	**Vă rog să îmi dați ceva pentru …** [və rog sə imʲ 'daʦʲ ʧe'va 'pentru …]
a headache	**durere de cap** [du'rere de kap]
a cough	**tuse** ['tuse]
a cold	**răceală** [rə'ʧalə]
the flu	**gripă** ['gripə]

a fever	**febră** ['febrə]
a stomach ache	**durere de stomac** [du'rere de sto'mak]
nausea	**greață** [grʲaʦə]
diarrhea	**diaree** [dia'ree]
constipation	**constipație** [konsti'paʦie]

pain in the back	**durere de spate** [du'rere de 'spate]
chest pain	**durere în piept** [du'rere în pjept]
side stitch	**junghi lateral** [ʒungi late'ral]
abdominal pain	**durere abdominală** [du'rere abdomi'nalə]

pill	**pastilă** [pas'tilə]
ointment, cream	**unguent, cremă** [ungu'ent, 'kremə]
syrup	**sirop** [si'rop]
spray	**spray** [spraj]
drops	**dropsuri** [dropsur]

You need to go to the hospital.	**Trebuie să mergeți la spital.** [trebuje sə mer'dʒets la spi'tal]
health insurance	**asigurare de sănătate** [asigu'rare de sənə'tate]
prescription	**rețetă** [re'tsetə]
insect repellant	**produs anti insecte** [pro'dus 'anti in'sektə]
Band Aid	**plasture** ['plasture]

The bare minimum

Excuse me, ...	**Nu vă supărați, ...** [nu və supə'ratsʲ, ...]
Hello.	**Buna ziua.** [buna 'ziwa]
Thank you.	**Mulțumesc.** [multsu'mesk]
Good bye.	**La revedere.** [la reve'dere]
Yes.	**Da.** [da]
No.	**Nu.** [nu]
I don't know.	**Nu știu.** [nu 'ʃtiu]
Where?	Where to?	When?	**Unde?	Încotro?	Când?** [unde?	ɨnko'tro?	kɨnd?]

I need ...	**Am nevoie de ...** [am ne'voje de ...]
I want ...	**Vreau ...** [vrʲau ...]
Do you have ...?	**Aveți ...?** [a'vetsʲ ...?]
Is there a ... here?	**Există ... aici?** [e'gzistə ... a'itʃi?]
May I ...?	**Pot ...?** [pot ...?]
..., please (polite request)	**..., vă rog** [..., və rog]

I'm looking for ...	**Caut ...** [kaut ...]
the restroom	**o toaletă** [o toa'letə]
an ATM	**un bancomat** [un banko'mat]
a pharmacy (drugstore)	**o farmacie** [o farma'tʃie]
a hospital	**un spital** [un spi'tal]
the police station	**o secție de poliție** [o 'sektsie de po'litsie]
the subway	**un metrou** [un me'trou]

a taxi	un taxi
	[un ta'ksi]
the train station	o gară
	[o 'garə]

My name is …	Numele meu este …
	[numele 'meu 'este …]
What's your name?	Cum vă numiți?
	[kum və nu'mitsʲ?]
Could you please help me?	Mă puteți ajuta, vă rog?
	[mə pu'tetsʲ aʒu'ta, və rog?]
I've got a problem.	Am o problemă.
	[am o pro'blemə]
I don't feel well.	Mi-e rău.
	[mi-e 'rəu]
Call an ambulance!	Chemați o ambulanță!
	[ke'matsʲ o ambu'lantsə!]
May I make a call?	Pot să dau un telefon?
	[pot sə dau un tele'fon?]

I'm sorry.	Îmi pare rău.
	[imʲ 'pare rəu]
You're welcome.	Cu plăcere.
	[ku plə'tʃere]

I, me	Eu
	[eu]
you (inform.)	tu
	[tu]
he	el
	[el]
she	ea
	[ja]
they (masc.)	ei
	[ej]
they (fem.)	ele
	['ele]
we	noi
	[noj]
you (pl)	voi
	[voj]
you (sg, form.)	dumneavoastră
	[dumnʲavo'astrə]

ENTRANCE	INTRARE
	[in'trare]
EXIT	IEȘIRE
	[je'ʃire]
OUT OF ORDER	DEFECT
	[de'fekt]
CLOSED	ÎNCHIS
	[in'kis]

OPEN

DESCHIS
[des'kis]

FOR WOMEN

PENTRU FEMEI
[pentru fe'mej]

FOR MEN

PENTRU BĂRBAȚI
[pentru bər'batsʲ]

MINI DICTIONARY

This section contains 250
useful words required for
everyday communication.
You will find the names of
months and days of the week
here. The dictionary also
contains topics such as colors,
measurements, family, and
more

T&P Books Publishing

DICTIONARY CONTENTS

T&P Books Publishing

time	**timp** (m)	[timp]
hour	**oră** (f)	['orə]
half an hour	**jumătate de oră**	[ʒumə'tate de 'orə]
minute	**minut** (n)	[mi'nut]
second	**secundă** (f)	[se'kundə]

today (adv)	**astăzi**	['astəzʲ]
tomorrow (adv)	**mâine**	['mɨjne]
yesterday (adv)	**ieri**	[jerʲ]

Monday	**luni** (f)	[lunʲ]
Tuesday	**marți** (f)	['martsʲ]
Wednesday	**miercuri** (f)	['merkurʲ]
Thursday	**joi** (f)	[ʒoj]
Friday	**vineri** (f)	['vinerʲ]
Saturday	**sâmbătă** (f)	['sɨmbətə]
Sunday	**duminică** (f)	[du'minikə]

day	**zi** (f)	[zi]
working day	**zi** (f) **de lucru**	[zi de 'lukru]
public holiday	**zi** (f) **de sărbătoare**	[zi de sərbəto'are]
weekend	**zile** (f pl) **de odihnă**	['zile de o'dihnə]

week	**săptămână** (f)	[səptə'mɨnə]
last week (adv)	**săptămâna trecută**	[səptə'mɨna tre'kutə]
next week (adv)	**săptămâna viitoare**	[səptə'mɨna viito'are]

| in the morning | **dimineața** | [dimi'nʲatsa] |
| in the afternoon | **după masă** | ['dupə 'masə] |

| in the evening | **seara** | ['sʲara] |
| tonight (this evening) | **astă-seară** | ['astə 'sʲarə] |

| at night | **noaptea** | [no'aptʲa] |
| midnight | **miezul** (n) **nopții** | ['mezul 'noptsij] |

January	**ianuarie** (m)	[janu'arie]
February	**februarie** (m)	[febru'arie]
March	**martie** (m)	['martie]
April	**aprilie** (m)	[a'prilie]
May	**mai** (m)	[maj]
June	**iunie** (m)	['junie]

| July | **iulie** (m) | ['julie] |
| August | **august** (m) | ['august] |

September	septembrie (m)	[sep'tembrie]
October	octombrie (m)	[ok'tombrie]
November	noiembrie (m)	[no'embrie]
December	decembrie (m)	[de'tʃembrie]

in spring	primăvara	[primə'vara]
in summer	vara	['vara]
in fall	toamna	[to'amna]
in winter	iarna	['jarna]

month	lună (f)	['lunə]
season (summer, etc.)	sezon (n)	[se'zon]
year	an (m)	[an]

2. Numbers. Numerals

0 zero	zero	['zero]
1 one	unu	['unu]
2 two	doi	[doj]
3 three	trei	[trej]
4 four	patru	['patru]

5 five	cinci	[tʃintʃ]
6 six	şase	['ʃase]
7 seven	şapte	['ʃapte]
8 eight	opt	[opt]
9 nine	nouă	['nowə]
10 ten	zece	['zetʃe]

11 eleven	unsprezece	['unsprezetʃe]
12 twelve	doisprezece	['dojsprezetʃe]
13 thirteen	treisprezece	['trejsprezetʃe]
14 fourteen	paisprezece	['pajsprezetʃe]
15 fifteen	cincisprezece	['tʃintʃsprezetʃe]

16 sixteen	şaisprezece	['ʃajsprezetʃe]
17 seventeen	şaptesprezece	['ʃaptesprezetʃe]
18 eighteen	optsprezece	['optsprezetʃe]
19 nineteen	nouăsprezece	['nowəsprezetʃe]

20 twenty	douăzeci	[dowə'zetʃi]
30 thirty	treizeci	[trej'zetʃi]
40 forty	patruzeci	[patru'zetʃi]
50 fifty	cincizeci	[tʃintʃ'zetʃ]

60 sixty	şaizeci	[ʃaj'zetʃi]
70 seventy	şaptezeci	[ʃapte'zetʃi]
80 eighty	optzeci	[opt'zetʃi]
90 ninety	nouăzeci	[nowə'zetʃi]
100 one hundred	o sută	[o 'sutə]

200 two hundred	**două sute**	['dowə 'sute]
300 three hundred	**trei sute**	[trej 'sute]
400 four hundred	**patru sute**	['patru 'sute]
500 five hundred	**cinci sute**	[tʃintʃ 'sute]
600 six hundred	**şase sute**	['ʃase 'sute]
700 seven hundred	**şapte sute**	['ʃapte 'sute]
800 eight hundred	**opt sute**	[opt 'sute]
900 nine hundred	**nouă sute**	['nowə 'sute]
1000 one thousand	**o mie**	[o 'mie]
10000 ten thousand	**zece mii**	['zetʃe mij]
one hundred thousand	**o sută de mii**	[o 'sutə de mij]
million	**milion** (n)	[mi'ljon]
billion	**miliard** (n)	[mi'ljard]

3. Humans. Family

man (adult male)	**bărbat** (m)	[bər'bat]
young man	**tânăr** (m)	['tinər]
woman	**femeie** (f)	[fe'meje]
girl (young woman)	**domnişoară** (f)	[domniʃo'arə]
old man	**bătrân** (m)	[bə'trin]
old woman	**bătrână** (f)	[bə'trinə]
mother	**mamă** (f)	['mamə]
father	**tată** (m)	['tatə]
son	**fiu** (m)	['fju]
daughter	**fiică** (f)	['fiikə]
brother	**frate** (m)	['frate]
sister	**soră** (f)	['sorə]
parents	**părinţi** (m pl)	[pə'rintsʲ]
child	**copil** (m)	[ko'pil]
children	**copii** (m pl)	[ko'pij]
stepmother	**mamă vitregă** (f)	['mamə 'vitregə]
stepfather	**tată vitreg** (m)	['tatə 'vitreg]
grandmother	**bunică** (f)	[bu'nikə]
grandfather	**bunic** (m)	[bu'nik]
grandson	**nepot** (m)	[ne'pot]
granddaughter	**nepoată** (f)	[nepo'atə]
grandchildren	**nepoţi** (m pl)	[ne'potsʲ]
uncle	**unchi** (m)	[unkʲ]
aunt	**mătuşă** (f)	[mə'tuʃə]
nephew	**nepot** (m)	[ne'pot]
niece	**nepoată** (f)	[nepo'atə]
wife	**soţie** (f)	[so'tsie]

husband	soţ (m)	[sots]
married (masc.)	căsătorit	[kəsəto'rit]
married (fem.)	căsătorită	[kəsəto'ritə]
widow	văduvă (f)	[vəduvə]
widower	văduv (m)	[vəduv]

| name (first name) | prenume (n) | [pre'nume] |
| surname (last name) | nume (n) | ['nume] |

relative	rudă (f)	['rudə]
friend (masc.)	prieten (m)	[pri'eten]
friendship	prietenie (f)	[priete'nie]

partner	partener (m)	[parte'ner]
superior (n)	director (m)	[di'rektor]
colleague	coleg (m)	[ko'leg]
neighbors	vecini (m pl)	[ve'tʃinʲ]

4. Human body

body	corp (n)	[korp]
heart	inimă (f)	['inimə]
blood	sânge (n)	['sɨndʒe]
brain	creier (m)	['krejer]

bone	os (n)	[os]
spine (backbone)	coloană (f) vertebrală	[kolo'anə verte'bralə]
rib	coastă (f)	[ko'astə]
lungs	plămâni (m pl)	[plə'mɨnʲ]
skin	piele (f)	['pjele]

head	cap (n)	[kap]
face	faţă (f)	['fatsə]
nose	nas (n)	[nas]
forehead	frunte (f)	['frunte]
cheek	obraz (m)	[o'braz]

mouth	gură (f)	['gurə]
tongue	limbă (f)	['limbə]
tooth	dinte (m)	['dinte]
lips	buze (f pl)	['buze]
chin	bărbie (f)	[bər'bie]

ear	ureche (f)	[u'reke]
neck	gât (n)	[gɨt]
eye	ochi (m)	[okʲ]
pupil	pupilă (f)	[pu'pilə]
eyebrow	sprânceană (f)	[sprɨn'tʃanə]
eyelash	geană (f)	['dʒanə]
hair	păr (m)	[pər]

hairstyle	coafură (f)	[koa'furə]
mustache	mustăţi (f pl)	[mus'tətsʲ]
beard	barbă (f)	['barbə]
to have (a beard, etc.)	a purta	[a pur'ta]
bald (adj)	chel	[kel]

hand	mână (f)	['mɨnə]
arm	braţ (n)	[brats]
finger	deget (n)	['dedʒet]
nail	unghie (f)	['ungie]
palm	palmă (f)	['palmə]

shoulder	umăr (m)	['umər]
leg	picior (n)	[pi'tʃior]
knee	genunchi (n)	[dʒe'nunkʲ]
heel	călcâi (n)	[kəl'kɨj]
back	spate (n)	['spate]

5. Clothing. Personal accessories

clothes	îmbrăcăminte (f)	[ɨmbrəkə'minte]
coat (overcoat)	palton (n)	[pal'ton]
fur coat	şubă (f)	['ʃubə]
jacket (e.g., leather ~)	scurtă (f)	['skurtə]
raincoat (trenchcoat, etc.)	trenci (f)	[trentʃi]

shirt (button shirt)	cămaşă (f)	[kə'maʃe]
pants	pantaloni (m pl)	[panta'lonʲ]
suit jacket	sacou (n)	[sa'kou]
suit	costum (n)	[kos'tum]

dress (frock)	rochie (f)	['rokie]
skirt	fustă (f)	['fustə]
T-shirt	tricou (n)	[tri'kou]
bathrobe	halat (n)	[ha'lat]
pajamas	pijama (f)	[piʒa'ma]
workwear	haină (f) de lucru	['hajnə de 'lukru]

underwear	lenjerie (f) de corp	[lenʒe'rie de 'korp]
socks	şosete (f pl)	[ʃo'sete]
bra	sutien (n)	[su'tjen]
pantyhose	ciorapi pantalon (m pl)	[tʃio'rapʲ panta'lon]
stockings (thigh highs)	ciorapi (m pl)	[tʃio'rapʲ]
bathing suit	costum (n) de baie	[kos'tum de 'bae]

hat	căciulă (f)	[kə'tʃiulə]
footwear	încălţăminte (f)	[ɨnkəltsə'minte]
boots (e.g., cowboy ~)	cizme (f pl)	['tʃizme]
heel	toc (n)	[tok]
shoestring	şiret (n)	[ʃi'ret]

shoe polish	cremă (f) de ghete	['kremə de 'gete]
gloves	mănuşi (f pl)	[mə'nuʃ]
mittens	mănuşi (f pl) cu un singur deget	[mə'nuʃ] ku un 'singur 'dedʒet]
scarf (muffler)	fular (m)	[fu'lar]
glasses (eyeglasses)	ochelari (m pl)	[oke'larʲ]
umbrella	umbrelă (f)	[um'brelə]
tie (necktie)	cravată (f)	[kra'vatə]
handkerchief	batistă (f)	[ba'tistə]
comb	pieptene (m)	['pjeptəne]
hairbrush	perie (f) de păr	[pe'rie de pər]
buckle	cataramă (f)	[kata'ramə]
belt	cordon (n)	[kor'don]
purse	poşetă (f)	[po'ʃətə]

6. House. Apartment

apartment	apartament (n)	[aparta'ment]
room	cameră (f)	['kamerə]
bedroom	dormitor (n)	[dormi'tor]
dining room	sufragerie (f)	[sufradʒe'rie]
living room	salon (n)	[sa'lon]
study (home office)	cabinet (n)	[kabi'net]
entry room	antreu (n)	[an'treu]
bathroom (room with a bath or shower)	baie (f)	['bae]
half bath	toaletă (f)	[toa'letə]
vacuum cleaner	aspirator (n)	[aspira'tor]
mop	teu (n)	['teu]
dust cloth	cârpă (f)	['kɨrpə]
short broom	mătură (f)	['məturə]
dustpan	făraş (n)	[fə'raʃ]
furniture	mobilă (f)	['mobilə]
table	masă (f)	['masə]
chair	scaun (n)	['skaun]
armchair	fotoliu (n)	[fo'tolju]
mirror	oglindă (f)	[og'lində]
carpet	covor (n)	[ko'vor]
fireplace	şemineu (n)	[ʃəmi'neu]
drapes	draperii (f pl)	[drape'rij]
table lamp	lampă (f) de birou	['lampə de bi'rou]
chandelier	lustră (f)	['lustrə]
kitchen	bucătărie (f)	[bukətə'rie]
gas stove (range)	aragaz (n)	[ara'gaz]

| electric stove | plită (f) electrică | ['plitə e'lektrikə] |
| microwave oven | cuptor (n) cu microunde | [kup'tor ku mikro'unde] |

refrigerator	frigider (n)	[fridʒi'der]
freezer	congelator (n)	[kondʒela'tor]
dishwasher	maşină (f) de spălat vase	[ma'ʃinə de spə'lat 'vase]
faucet	robinet (n)	[robi'net]

meat grinder	maşină (f) de tocat carne	[ma'ʃinə de to'kat 'karne]
juicer	storcător (n)	[storkə'tor]
toaster	prăjitor (n) de pâine	[prəʒi'tor de 'pɨne]
mixer	mixer (n)	['mikser]

coffee machine	fierbător (n) de cafea	[fierbə'tor de ka'fʲa]
kettle	ceainic (n)	['ʧajnik]
teapot	ceainic (n)	['ʧajnik]

TV set	televizor (n)	[televi'zor]
VCR (video recorder)	videomagnetofon (n)	[videomagneto'fon]
iron (e.g., steam ~)	fier (n) de călcat	[fier de kəl'kat]
telephone	telefon (n)	[tele'fon]

Printed in Great Britain
by Amazon